contents

65. STAND OF DREAMS

YOU GUYS WERE GREAT!

CHATTER

CHATTER

HEY!

IT'S SUZUKI!

WAH!

CHATTER

10

IT'S OFFICIAL, NOW! YOU'RE OUR FIRST-YEAR ACE!

AFTER WE'D SEEN YOU HOLD THEM BACK FOR THE REST OF THE GAME, THOUGH, YOU SHOULD'VE HEARD HOW LOUD WE GOT IN THE STANDS.

UH...

I THOUGHT WE WERE DONE FOR WHEN THEY SCORED ALL THOSE RUNS AT ONCE, BUT DAMN!

YOU WERE AMAZING OUT THERE!

WOW, SUZUKI.

YOU'RE POPULAR ALL OF A SUDDEN.

WAAAA

IF WE CAN KEEP THIS UP, WE MIGHT EVEN MAKE IT TO THE NATIONAL CHAMPIONSHIP THIS YEAR, HUH?

IT'S GONNA BE A NEW ERA FOR THE KANAN BASEBALL CLUB!

WAAAA

HE MAY HAVE QUIT THE TEAM BEFORE THIS DO-OVER, BUT I GUESS HE'S GOT A GIFT FOR BASEBALL AFTER ALL.

I WAS THINKING—

UH... SO...

WHAT?

OH MY GOD! ♥ THERE HE IS!

HEY, IMA-MURA-KUN.

9

1

0

ATTEN-
TION!

BUT OUR BASE-BALL TEAM PUT UP ONE HELL OF A FIGHT, AND I'D SAY YOU GUYS DID YOUR HONEST BEST.

WE LOST.

WELL...

NOD

RIGHT?

MR. PRINCI-PAL?

THE OUEN-DAN'S DOING WELL.

PLEASE KEEP IT UP.

BADUMP

USAMI!

THEY PROBABLY LIKE YOU WELL ENOUGH.

HMM?

BESIDES, WHO KNOWS WHAT THE OTHER STUDENTS THINK OF US?

FIDGET

FIDGET

BUT SIR...

WE DID LOSE.

THE WHOLE TEAM IS DYING TO TAKE A PICTURE WITH YOU GUYS.

HEY.

CAP-TAIN?

HUH?

LOOK-ING GOOD!

SMILE!

MAKE A PEACE SIGN, YOU GUYS!

HERE WE GO!

OKAY!

OKAY, NOW SAY CHEESE!

SNAP

YOU SHOULD CHEER US ON LIKE THAT AT THE NATIONAL CHAMPIONSHIP!

IT WAS FUN WATCHING YOU CHEER!

THANKS FOR EVERYTHING!

WE'RE COUNTING ON YOU, USAMI!

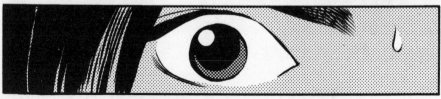

GET IN THE PICTURE.

COME ON.

BADUMP
ビキッ

USAMI-SAN!

SNAP

... ...

WE'RE PRACTICING MORE NEXT TIME.

HMPH.

FLINCH

USAMI!

SNAP!!

Osu! Please shake my hand!

Huh?

Huh?

May I take a picture with you as well?

Osu!

I'll upload this to Facebook.

YOU EVEN HAVE SOME FANS IN OUR OWN. YOU ALWAYS HAVE.

WELL USAMI, IT APPEARS YOU'VE BECOME A FINE CAPTAIN TO YOUR OUENDAN.

IWA-SAKI...

DB DADUMP

...I FELL FOR YOU ALL OVER AGAIN.

TODAY...

CHI-CHAN!

Again!!

アゲイン!!

PARTY'S OVER...

SNAP

SNAP

MOM, WHAT DO YOU THINK YOU'RE DOING?

...

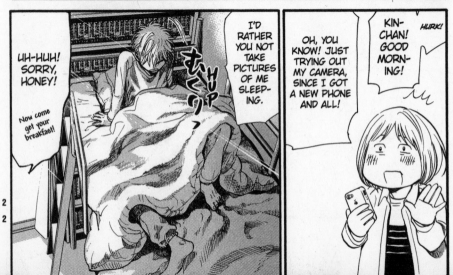

UH-HUH! SORRY, HONEY!

Now come get your breakfast!

I'D RATHER YOU NOT TAKE PICTURES OF ME SLEEPING.

HUP

OH, YOU KNOW! JUST TRYING OUT MY CAMERA, SINCE I GOT A NEW PHONE AND ALL!

KIN-CHAN! GOOD MORN-ING!

HURK!

I'LL BE BACK AROUND SIX.

OH, NAH.

I'M GOING TO BE HOME A LITTLE LATE TONIGHT. WHEN WILL YOU BE BACK, KIN-CHAN?

DO YOU MIND WAITING FOR DINNER?

OH! BY THE WAY...

YOU MUST MEAN THOSE SQUEALING LADIES...

OH YEAH...

HUH?

So, hey! These are my new friends. They're all fans of yours! ♡

Kin-chan! ♡ I came after all!

I'VE NEVER SEEN ONE BEFORE, SO THEY'RE TAKING ME! ♡

APPARENTLY, THE OTHER MOMS I MET AT THAT GAME YOU CHEERED AT ARE INTO TAKARAZUKA MUSICALS!

THESE ARE THE FIRST MOM FRIENDS I'VE MADE SINCE MOVING HERE.

I OWE YOU ONE, KIN-CHAN.

NICE.

I'M HAPPY FOR YOU.

SAITAMA PREFECTURE KABOSU MINAMI HIGH SCHOOL

2
5

HEY.

MORNING, IMAMURA.

NICE HAIRCUT, REO! IT'S SO CUTE.

YOU THINK?

HEY.

GOOD MORNING, IMAMURA. ♥

WHO ARE THEY?

ぼへっ
えへっ

HEY.

GOOD MORNING.

GOOD MORNING, IMAMURA!

MORNING.

YOU'VE SEEMED OFF SINCE THE PRACTICE GAME.

I'VE BEEN WONDERING, TOO.

HEY, REO. ARE YOU, LIKE, AVOIDING IMAMURA NOW?

DID SOMETHING HAPPEN?

...

SHUF

NO.

NOT REALLY.

NOW I FEEL LIKE A FOOL FOR TAKING HER SERIOUSLY.

DAMN.

I WANT TO GET CLOSE WITH YOU AGAIN, LIKE THE OLD DAYS!

YOU WANT TO TALK TO **ME**?

WHY NOT TALK TO THE CAPTAIN?

THERE'S SOME STUFF I WANT TO TALK TO YOU ABOUT.

HEY, SO I WAS WONDERING. WANNA GRAB A BITE SOMEWHERE ON OUR WAY HOME?

ONE AND TWO AND THREE AND FOUR!

HMM?

G-GOD!

TALK TO SOMEBODY ELSE ABOUT IT.

MY HANDS ARE PRETTY FULL WITH MY OWN STUFF RIGHT NOW.

ACTUALLY,

PANT PANT PANT

IMA-MURA!

WHEEZE PAANT

I SEE YOU SPACING OUT!

FWISH!

DASH!!

OSU!

...BUT IN THE END, THE OUENDAN SURVIVED.

OH, LOOK!

IT'S THOSE OUENDAN KIDS!

WE LOST THE GAME...

TRAIN HARD! YOU GUYS!

WHEEZE

DO IT RIGHT.

YELL!

SO DO I REALLY HAVE THE RIGHT TO KEEP DOING THIS?

I COULDN'T BELIEVE IN SUZUKI THROUGH TO THE VERY END, THOUGH...

SNAP

TUP

TUP

TUP

TUP

MAYBE WE WOULDN'T LOSE IF IT WEREN'T FOR ME.

...WHAT AM I SAYING?

MAYBE IT'S TRUE.

?

KITAJIMA SENSEI!

I'VE GOT NEWS FOR YOU!

BIG NEWS!

HEEEY!

USAMI!

HUH ?!

THERE WERE THREE OF THEM!

I JUST GOT A VISIT...

...FROM SOME STUDENTS HOPING TO JOIN THE OUENDAN!

THEY SAID THEY'VE ADMIRED YOU GUYS SINCE THE PRACTICE GAME!

ISN'T THAT GREAT ?

THEY DIDN'T SEEM QUITE READY TO COMMIT, BUT THEY'RE WILLING TO HELP US OUT UNTIL THE BASEBALL TOURNAMENT THIS SUMMER!

TWO GIRLS AND A BOY.

BLUUUSH

NO MAN WILL TAKE YOU FROM ME!

IT'S GOTTEN WORSE.

SOMEBODY'S EXCITED.

GASP

WHAT'S WITH THAT FACE, IMAMURA?

THEY ADMIRE US, HUH?

REALLY?

MELT

AWWW, WHAT?

MELT

IT'S NOTHING... NOTHING AT ALL...

I GOT WHAT I WANTED OUT OF THIS DO-OVER...

...SO WHAT'S BOTHERING ME SO MUCH?!

HEH HEH HEH HEH

WHY ARE YOU LURKING OVER THERE, HI-RO-KUN?

HEH HEH HEH HEH

NOW YOU'RE ACTING ALL HIGH-AND-MIGHTY LIKE YOU'RE THE ONLY PERSON IN THE WORLD WHO MATTERS, AND I DON'T GET WHY!

NO!

THE HIRO-KUN I KNOW IS GOOD AT BOOK LEARNING BUT CAN'T APPLY ANY OF IT! HE ACTS LIKE HE'S ALL SMART AND COOL BUT HE'S ACTUALLY JUST A BIG DOOFUS!

EVEN IF I KEPT GOING, IT'S NOT LIKE I EVER GOT ON OUR TEAM'S STARTING LINEUP!

SHUT UP!

SOCCER USED TO BE ALL YOU CARED ABOUT! REMEM—

YOU'VE BEEN SKIPPING SOCCER PRACTICE LATELY, TOO.

WHAT HAPPENED?

FWSH

HUH ...?

THAT WAS BEFORE THE DO-OVER.

HOW ...?

HIRO-KUN ...

STUFF LIKE THAT DOESN'T HAPPEN IN REAL LIFE! DOES IT?

I'D PROBABLY LOSE IT IF I KNEW THE FUTURE! NOOO! I'M SO SCARED!

AKI! GO GET ME A SHRIMP-AND-MAYO RICE BALL FROM THE CORNER STORE...

THAT MIGHT HELP MY HEAD STOP HURTING.

RIGHT! ON IT! JUST WAIT THERE!

DASH

OF COURSE, THAT'S JUST A GUESS...

WHAT'S GOING ON? IS OUR DO-OVER CHANGING SPACE-TIME ITSELF? MAYBE HIRO-KUN'S MEMORIES FROM NOW AND THREE YEARS IN THE FUTURE GOT LINKED TOGETHER SOMEHOW...

HE MIGHT DIE OF SHOCK IF I TELL HIM ABOUT THIS STUFF, THOUGH.

AGH!

THINGS WERE ABOUT TO GET COMPLI-CATED. THAT WAS CLOSE.

...

I'M DOING THINGS OVER, TOO.

BUT I THINK I'LL KEEP THAT MY LITTLE SECRET FOR NOW.

I'LL BE RIGHT BACK!

See ya!

IMA- MURA! WE'RE IN THE MIDDLE OF PRAC- TICE!

GET OVER HERE.

STOP IT!

DRAG

DRAG

IT STILL FEELS LIKE A DREAM TO ME.

I'M LOOKING INTO WHETHER WE'VE ACTUALLY GONE THREE YEARS BACK IN TIME FROM 2014 OR WHAT.

I'M NOT SURE IF THIS IS REALLY THE PAST.

DO YOU HAVE A WAY BACK?

HOW DID YOU GET HERE, HIRO-KUN?

WHAT'S HAPPENED TO ME IN THE WORLD WE'RE FROM?!

THEN I'LL TELL YOU.

AAAAAGH

YOU REALLY WANT TO KNOW?

IMA-MURA!

ACK!

WHOA.

YOU'RE USELESS.

I HAVE NO IDEA WHAT HAPPENED TO YOU!

SO, I FELL OUT THE WINDOW RIGHT AFTER YOU DID, AND NEXT THING I KNEW, HERE I WAS.

HEH HEH HEH

AAA A AA

I AM.

HEH HEH HEH

ARE YOU PLANNING SOMETHING?

WAIT, IF YOU FELL RIGHT AFTER I DID, HAVE YOU BEEN HIDING IT SINCE BEFORE THE PRACTICE GAME?

UGH!

G-GUUH...

LISTEN, IMAMURA.

MY HEAD IS CRAMMED FULL OF INFO THAT I MEMORIZED FOR WHEN I GOT MY OWN DO-OVER.

THE OUENDAN ISN'T WHERE YOU BELONG.

THIS IS OUR CHANCE TO DO THINGS OVER AGAIN.

LET'S TAKE THIS BORING WORLD AND LEAVE OUR MARK ON IT.

LET'S BLOW IT ALL UP!

BOOOOM

DRAMATIC REENACTMENT

GOD, HIRO-KUN!

HEY! THERE YOU ARE!

HOW EXACTLY IS KNOWING THE FUTURE SUPPOSED TO HELP US?

UGH, GUH...

YOU THINK WE CAN START A NUCLEAR WAR OR END THE WORLD JUST 'CAUSE WE'RE DOING THINGS OVER? HUH? COOL YOUR HEAD! YOU'RE STILL JUST SOME HIGH-SCHOOLER.

GET REAL!

OH YEAH. COULDN'T YOU BE NICER?

YOU'RE THE ONE WHO WANTED TO GO OUT IN THE FIRST PLACE!

AND YOU'VE BEEN ACTING ALL BORED ON OUR DATES!

WHY HAVEN'T YOU REPLIED TO MY TEXT FROM YESTERDAY?

WHAT?!

LET'S BREAK UP.

YOU TURNED OUT TOO BORING FOR ME.

...

AND WE'VE ONLY BEEN DATING FOR THREE DAYS, YET SHE WANTS THE WHOLE GIRLFRIEND EXPERIENCE. I CAN'T STAND IT.

SHE JUST KEEPS BLABBERING ON AND ON. IT'S WORSE THAN I EXPECTED.

YOU SUCK! YOU ASSHOLE! YOU'RE THE WORST!

SHUT UP! ANYONE ELSE WOULD DO THE SAME!

Is this what you mean by "leaving your mark"?

HIRO-KUN.

THIS DO-OVER TURNED YOU INTO A REAL *PIECE OF SHIT*, DIDN'T IT?

WHAT DO YOU WANT TO DO, IMAMURA? I CAN HELP MAKE IT HAPPEN.

A LOT OF MONEY COULD BE NICE.

MONEY, I GUESS?

HEY, USAMI! I'M HEADING HOME!

WHERE ARE YOU?

HIRO-KUUUN! I BOUGHT THAT SHRIMP-AND-MAYO RICE BALL FOR YOU!

WHAT THE HELL?!

SIGN: URAWA HORSE RACES

BESIDES, HAVE YOU REALLY MEMORIZED THE RESULTS OF EVERY RACE?

I MEAN, WE'RE HIGH-SCHOOLERS. ARE WE EVEN *ALLOWED* TO BET ON HORSES?

CLANG
CLANG

DAMN IT! I GUESS THEY DON'T START THAT UNTIL NEXT YEAR.

THERE'S SUPPOSED TO BE A PLACE FOR OFF-TRACK BETTING HERE.

YEAH, 'CAUSE WE HAVE ALL THAT MONEY TO INVEST.

WELL, THERE'S STOCK TRADING.

...

EVEN FOR BETTING ON SOCCER GAMES?

I'M PRETTY SURE MINORS USUALLY AREN'T ALLOWED TO BUY THOSE. LIKE, WE'D NEED OUR PARENTS' PERMISSION OR SOMETHING?

LET'S BUY LOTTERY TICKETS! I TOOK A LOOK AT THE WINNING NUMBERS!

WE'RE GONNA HOLD ANOTHER STRATEGY MEETING ON OUR PLANS FOR THIS DO-OVER TOMORROW. COME PREPARED!

IT'S THE MIDDLE OF THE NIGHT! WHERE WERE YOU?

HEY! KIN-CHAN!

WHY DIDN'T YOU TELL ME YOU'D BE HOME LATE?!

WHAT WOULD YOU DO IF WE WERE RICH?

MOM.

OH. ATSUKO MAEDA, HUH? SHE'LL RETIRE NEXT YEAR.

JUST KIDDING.

NO WAY!

JUST KIDDING.

KIN-CHAN! I DID NOT RAISE YOU TO BE A CRIMINAL!

WHAM

USING THIS DO-OVER FOR MY OWN BENEFIT, HUH?

I HADN'T THOUGHT OF THAT.

HE AND I MAY AS WELL HAVE BEEN FROM DIFFERENT WORLDS.

HE WAS SOME LOUD, ANNOYING GUY, ALWAYS YUKKING IT UP WITH HIS CARBON-COPY BUDDIES FROM OUR WEAK-ASS SOCCER TEAM, LIKE THEY WERE MAKING FUN OF SOMEBODY.

WHAT WAS MY IMPRESSION OF "HIRO-KUN" BEFORE I JUMPED BACK IN TIME?

68.   **DEVILISHLY CHARMING**

IT'S NOT AS SIMPLE AS JUST TRYING TO BE THE BEATLES BEFORE THE BEATLES!

WE KNOW WHAT SONGS ARE GOING TO BE HITS, SO WE CAN DO THEM OURSELVES FIRST AND SELL A TON OF CDS.

WHY NOT, THOUGH? WE'D MAKE SO MUCH MONEY!

LIKE, ARE YOU REALLY DUMB ENOUGH TO THINK A SONG BY AKB48 OR SOME BOY BAND LIKE EXILE WOULD SELL JUST AS WELL IF WE SANG IT?

I MEAN, WE COULD STEAL A POPULAR JOKE FROM THE FUTURE, AND NO ONE WOULD THINK IT WAS FUNNY. THE SAME GOES FOR MANGA, ANIME, MOVIES, AND BOOKS. WE MAY KNOW WHAT'S COMING, BUT WE CAN'T RECREATE IT, SO JUST GIVE UP ON THE ARTS ALREADY.

BAM

DAMN IT! AND IT'LL BE A WHILE BEFORE ANOTHER SILLY CHILDREN'S SONG MAKES THE CHARTS, LIKE THAT ONE ABOUT THE DUMPLINGS...

GAAAH! SORRY!

WHAT ARE YOU PLANNING? YOU'RE SUPPOSED TO BE IN CLASS!

OH?

I WANT TO GAMBLE ON A BASEBALL GAME OR SOMETHING!

AAAGH! IS THERE REALLY NO WAY TO MAKE SOME EASY MONEY?

MMMMGH

...

IMA-MURA?!

SHOOOO

JOLT

SCREW SCHOOL!

HA-HAAA!!

Usami-san! Pay attention to class!

HE'S STARTED DOWN THE WRONG PATH...

HE STOPS ATTENDING SCHOOL.
↓
THE COPS GET INVOLVED.
↓
HE BREAKS A BUNCH OF THE SCHOOL'S WINDOWS.
↓
THE OUENDAN IS DONE FOR.

HUUURK!

IMA-
MURA...

IS THIS
STILL
NOT GOOD
ENOUGH?

WHAT THE
HELL HAS
GOTTEN
INTO YOU,
IMAMURA?

ARE YOU
ASKING
TO GO
FURTHER
WITH ME?

IF WE
WANT TO
LEAVE THE
DO-OVER
WORLD AND
GET BACK TO
OUR OLD
ONE,

ANOTHER
SHOCK TO
THE HEAD
SHOULD BE
ENOUGH TO
DO IT, RIGHT?
HMM...

I MEAN,
I DON'T
KNOW IF
THIS IS A
PARALLEL
UNIVERSE
OR A
DREAM
OR WHAT,
BUT...

I WENT TO SCHOOL LIKE EVERYBODY ELSE, DID MY HOMEWORK LIKE EVERYBODY ELSE, JOINED A CLUB LIKE EVERYBODY ELSE...

THAT WAS HIGH SCHOOL FOR ME: DOING THE SAME THING AS EVERYBODY ELSE.

BUT I WANTED TO DO SOMETHING UNIQUE, SOMETHING NOBODY ELSE WAS CAPABLE OF!

I ALWAYS HAVE!

ワン WOOF

ワン WOOF

WOW, EVEN PEOPLE WITH LIVES HAVE THEIR PROBLEMS, HUH?

ワン WOOF

SORRY, CAN'T RELATE.

ワン WOOF

Whoa! I'm so sorry!

WAIT, YOU HAVE?!

THUMP THUMP THUMP THUMP

UGH! HGH!

JUMP

NO ...

...

WAG WAG WAG

ワン WOOF

IMA-MURA...

HAVE YOU EVER HAD SEX?

SO, WHICH ONE ARE YOU GONNA SCREW FIRST?

I'VE GOTTA HAND IT TO YOU. THAT'S AWESOME! YOU'RE REALLY MAKING THE MOST OF THIS DO-OVER, HUH?

THEN HAVE YOU EVER KISSED SOME-ONE?

LICK LICK LICK LICK LICK LICK

HA-HAAA!

YOU'VE ALREADY KISSED BOTH THE CAPTAIN *AND* SHIBATA?!

WHOA!

woof woof?!

They're virgins, right? You've gotta do 'em!

ANYWAY, I DON'T GET WHAT FUJIEDA SEES IN YOU.

JUST, I'M NOT USED TO THIS KIND OF LOCKER-ROOM TALK. I CAN'T THINK STRAIGHT...

NOTH-ING.

Hey. Hey.

WHY DO YOU LOOK SO HORRI-FIED?

SHE SURE ACTS LIKE YOUR GIRL-FRIEND.

YOU SAID YOU WEREN'T HER BOYFRIEND, RIGHT? WHAT DID YOU MEAN BY THAT?

I AM *NOT* AKI'S BOY-FRIEND.

AFTER ALL, SHE WAS COOL AND PEPPY AND SILLY, AND HER FACE WASN'T HALF-BAD EITHER.

FUJIEDA AND I WERE ASSIGNED TO THE SAME CLASS IN OUR SECOND YEAR. WE'D TALK PRETTY OFTEN, AND I CAME TO CONSIDER HER A FRIEND.

SO, I LIKED HER WELL ENOUGH.

BWA HA HA...

THEN ONE DAY, THE TWO OF US WERE CLOWNING AROUND ABOUT SOME-THING, AND...

I NEVER SAW HER AS GIRL-FRIEND MATERIAL.

BUT I'VE HAD A THING FOR OLDER WOMEN EVER SINCE THIS ONE GIRLFRIEND OF MINE, SO SHE DIDN'T QUITE DO IT FOR ME.

HAAAAA

I'm dying!

THAT'S WHAT I LOVE ABOUT YOU.

DAMN, FUJI-EDA.

FROM THEN UNTIL WE GRADUATED, EVERYONE SAW ME AS HER BOYFRIEND.

God, you guys don't have to tell everyone! It's embarrassing!

Huh?!

Huh?!

We heard the news!

You two make a good match.

THE NEXT DAY, I WENT TO SCHOOL TO FIND THAT OUR WHOLE CLASS SAW US AS A COUPLE NOW.

KICK

KICK

AAAGH!

...

I SHOULD'VE JUST BROKEN UP WITH HER WHILE I HAD THE CHANCE.

SO, BUSY AS I WAS WITH THE SOCCER CLUB AND MY SCHOOL WORK, I GOT STUCK PRETENDING TO BE HER BOYFRIEND.

AND BECAUSE OF THAT, ALL THE GIRLS CONSIDERED ME OFF-LIMITS.

BUT HERE I AM DOING THINGS OVER, AND THIS TIME, I'M GOING TO HAVE SOME FUN WITH A WOMAN MORE TO MY LIKING!

FWISH

YOU BETTER NOT LET FUJIEDA CATCH WIND OF THAT.

WHEN YOU'RE SO STRAIT-LACED YOU CAN'T STEP OUTSIDE YOUR COMFORT ZONE,

YOU'RE EVENTUALLY GONNA EXPLODE. I WAS ALWAYS NERVOUS ABOUT THAT.

WHAT? NO YOU WEREN'T.

I THOUGHT YOU WERE PRETTY STRAIT-LACED, BUT I GUESS I WAS WRONG.

YOU KNOW,

I'M SORRY, I'M JUST NOT READY...

YOU PROMISED WE'D DO IT WHEN YOU GRADUATED, BABE.

WHATEVER! COME ON, REO.

OH!

COME TO THINK OF IT, AFTER OUR GRADUATION, SHE WAS ON THE VERGE OF LETTING SOME DOUCHEBAG DRAG HER INTO A LOVE HOTEL.

SEE?

HUH?

TAKE SHIBATA. SHE'S EXACTLY THE TYPE.

THIS IS A DO-OVER, AFTER ALL. YOU SHOULD DO WHAT YOU WANT TO.

NO?

...

COME ON, YOU DON'T HAVE TO DO AS YOU'RE TOLD LIKE A GOOD LITTLE BOY.

...

AND I BET YOU'VE BEEN GETTING BORED OF THE STRAIT-LACED OUENDAN LIFE YOURSELF, HAVEN'T YOU?

...

M—

WEAK.

GOD.

EVERYONE'S SUCH CREEPS!

I THINK I'VE FIGURED OUT WHAT'S BEEN BOTHERING ME LATELY.

PEOPLE JUST DECIDE WHAT I WANT AND WHAT TO EXPECT FROM ME WITHOUT EVEN ASKING. NOBODY WONDERS WHAT I MIGHT WANT!

OH, IMA-MURA-KUN...

WHAT IF...

I'LL GO LOOK FOR HIM.

LUMBER

IMA-MURA-KUN!

...HE'S SKIPPING SCHOOL BECAUSE OF ME?!

I can't go to school with her there!

...WHAT DID YOU WANT TO TALK ABOUT?

SO...

OOF...

BA DUMP

...

SHE KNOWS...

IS THIS GOOD NEWS?

OR BAD NEWS?

FIRST...

HMMM. UHHH...

HELL, MAYBE IT'D BE BEST TO MAKE HER HATE ME.

I KNOW I'M JUST GOING TO DISAPPOINT HER, SO WE SHOULD QUIT WHILE WE'RE AHEAD. BUT HOW DO I TELL HER THAT?

I DON'T WANT TO GET HER HOPES UP...

GET REAL, NERD.

I CAN'T BELIEVE YOU TOOK THAT KISS SERIOUSLY.

WHAT?

IF YOU'RE NOT INTERESTED, JUST SAY SO, OKAY?

IF—

FSSH!!!

...TO DISNEYLAND?

WANNA COME WITH ME...

OOH AH...

WHA—

AH—

?

WHY NOT JUST GO WITH A FRIEND?

MY MOM GOT THESE FROM ONE OF HER CO-WORKERS. IT WAS A COINCIDENCE! SHE GAVE THEM TO ME, AND THERE ARE ONLY TWO, SO I FIGURED, YOU KNOW... MIGHT AS WELL...

HUH?

I WANT TO GO ...

...WITH YOU.

RIGHT.

OH-HH-HH.

OH.

I MEAN, ONLY IF YOU WANT TO.

WHAAAT?!

LET'S GO RIGHT NOW.

IT'D BE TOO CROWDED IF WE WENT ON THE WEEK-END.

HUH?!

HURK

LET'S GO, THEN.

CARS

A-ARE YOU SURE THE POLICE WON'T BOTHER US IF WE GO IN OUR UNIFORMS?

EH.

DON'T ACT SO NERVOUS.

I BET THERE ARE PLENTY OF STUDENTS OUT ON FIELD TRIPS.

IMAMURA! WHAT'S GOTTEN INTO YOU?

WHY'S HE SO ASSERTIVE ALL OF A SUDDEN?

WHOA, WHOA, WHOA, WHAT?!

ドキ ドキ ドキ ドキ
BADUMP BADUMP BADUMP BADUMP

...YOU'RE TAKING ME ON THE FIRST DATE OF MY ENTIRE LIFE!

トO TOOT

I MEAN...

ガタタッ
RAAATTLE

ガタタ タ
RAAATTLE

ガタ ン
RATTLE

ガタン
RATTLE

ガタン...
RATTLE

ガタ
RATTLE

ゴト
RATTLE

HOW MANY TRANSFERS DO WE HAVE TO MAKE, AGAIN?

THIS IS TAKING A WHILE.

HE SEEMS MOODY, BUT WHY?!

IMAMURA-KUN...

DOES HE NOT ACTUALLY WANT TO GO? OH, GOD...

RATTLE RATTLE

I-I CAN PAY YOUR FARE.

DON'T SWEAT IT.

THREE TRANSFERS. THE TRIP THERE WILL TAKE AN HOUR AND FORTY MINUTES AND COST 1,100 YEN.

S-S-S-SORRY!

BUT TODAY, I'M MAKING IT MY JOB TO ACT MOODY AND COMPLETELY UNINTERESTED IN DISNEYLAND!

SORRY, SHIBATA.

I DON'T THINK I LIKE YOU, IMAMURA.

THIS WASN'T REALLY WHAT I EXPECTED.

THAT WAY, SHIBATA SHOULD BE OVER HER SILLY CRUSH BY THE TIME WE'RE READY TO LEAVE.

THE CONVERSATION WILL BE SO BORING, AND I CAN GO ON ABOUT THE EVILS OF CONSUMERISM TO REALLY PUT HER OFF.

I'LL COMPLAIN ABOUT THE LONG LINES AND THE EXPENSIVE FOOD, STUFF LIKE THAT.

HURRRR

HURK

FART

FART

FART

FINISH!!

HNNNGH ぐッぬッ

HEH HEH...

I'M REALLY LOOKING FORWARD TO THIS.

ちらッ GLANCE

ゴ SHOOOOOO

THINK EVIL THOUGHTS. NO NO NO!

I'VE GOT TO MAKE HER HATE ME!

東京...ランド・パーク
Tokyo Disneyland Park →

...シー・パーク
(トレインのりかえ)

CHATTER

CHATTER

DAMN, IT'S RAINING CATS AND DOGS.

PERFECT! NOW I CAN GET EVEN MOODIER!

CLENCH

DON'T YOU WANNA CHECK IT OUT?

WHAT'S UP, SHIBATA?

MAYBE I WENT TOO FAR...

TURN

WE'RE GONNA GET SOAKED WAITING IN LINE.

WE DON'T EVEN HAVE AN UMBRELLA.

GOD, I HATE RAIN. THIS SUCKS.

SHIVER

UGH.

SHIVER

OH, DON'T GO OUT OF YOUR WAY FOR ME.

I'M SORRY. LET'S GO HOME. I'LL PAY FOR YOUR FARE FOR THE TRAIN.

SORRY FOR THE TROUBLE.

I'M JUST MAKING YOU TAG ALONG WITH ME, AND IT'S NOT LIKE WE'LL EVEN HAVE ANY FUN IN ALL THIS RAIN.

IT'S FINE, IMAMURA-KUN. I CAN TELL YOU AREN'T INTERESTED.

COME ON, WE CAN JUST BUY AN UMBRELLA.

SHI-BATA!

BESIDES, THE LINES WILL BE SHORTER IF IT'S RAINING.

SHAKE SHAKE

MM...

MM...

DAMN IT... WHAT CAN I DO?

GWUH!

UU-UNH...

UNH...

GLINT

IN THAT CASE, LET'S GO SOME- WHERE I WANT TO GO.

WHERE DO YOU MEAN?

HUH ...?

OH, YEAH! THERE'S ONE IN SHIN- KIBA.

I WON- DER IF THERE'S ONE NEARBY.

THIS WAY.

YOU MUST BE HUNGRY, RIGHT?

YOU THINK YOU'RE TROUBLE?

I'LL SHOW YOU TROUBLE!

CAN I GET A SHRIMP AND AVOCADO SUB?

GIVE ME EXTRA VEGGIES, EXCEPT FOR LETTUCE.

AND HOW ABOUT SOME CHILI PEPPERS.

ON A SESAME BUN.

TOASTED, PLEASE.

WHAT DO YOU WANT, SHIBATA?

Hours 7:00 AM–9:00 PM

ONE MORE OF THE SAME, THEN.

I'LL JUST HAVE WHAT YOU'RE HAVING.

OH, UH... I DON'T REALLY KNOW HOW TO ORDER HERE.

WITH EXTRA OLIVES, PLEASE.

GASP

YOU MADE YOUR ORDER LIKE IT WAS NO BIG DEAL.

YOU'RE AMAZING, IMAMURA-KUN.

WE'D ONLY DO THAT ONCE IN A WHILE, THOUGH.

MY DAD WOULD TAKE ME. HE'S THE ONE WHO TAUGHT ME HOW TO ORDER.

YEAH, I CAME HERE A LOT WHEN I LIVED IN TOKYO.

WHAT HAPPENED TO MAKING HER HATE ME? I'VE GOTTEN TOO COMFORT-ABLE.

ガタン
CLATTER

...

NO NEED TO APOLO-GIZE.

ガタ...
CLATTER

OH...

SORRY...

I WOULDN'T SAY THAT. HE'S NOT IN THE PICTURE ANYMORE.

WOW, WHAT A GREAT DAD!

SO WHEN SHOULD WE...

...DO THAT THING?

JUST LET ME KNOW WHEN YOU'RE READY, OKAY?

IMA-MURA-KUN,

I WON'T ASK AGAIN.

OH...

RIGHT.

UHH...

...AND THAT WOULD BE THE END OF IT.

I THOUGHT WE WERE JUST GOING TO LET EACH OTHER KNOW HOW WE FELT...

...

O... KAY.

BUT SURPRISINGLY...

...I CAN'T HELP BUT ENJOY MYSELF.

NO WAY!

WHAT?

I FORGET.

WHAT WAS IT YOU WANTED TO TALK ABOUT EARLIER, IMAMURA-KUN?

OH, AND BY THE WAY,

LETTING THIS GO A LITTLE LONGER MIGHT NOT BE SO BAD.

THAT.

OHHH...

70. RED HOT CHERRY PEPPERS

I'LL FUCKIN' KILL YOU!

IT'S DANGEROUS TO TALK ON THE PHONE WHILE RIDING A BIKE.

YOU'RE THE OUEN-DAN'S CAPTAIN.

WAIT...

WHAT? I'M USING HIM?

YOU'RE USING HIM! AREN'T YOU? THAT MUST BE WHY HE'S STARTED SKIPPING PRACTICE!

YOU'RE THAT GUY WHO WAS WITH IMAMURA!

HM? YOU ARE...?

OF COURSE, I'M SURE YOU GOT IT IN YOUR HEAD THAT HE'D CARRY ON THE OUENDAN YOU'VE WORKED SO HARD TO PRESERVE.

DON'T YOU REAL- IZE?

HE'S JUST GETTING SICK OF YOU.

HE'S AL- READY LOSING IN- TEREST.

カララー...
WHIRRR

IMAMURA'S PERFECTLY HAPPY FOR THE OUENDAN TO GO ON WITHOUT HIM.

THE THING IS,

YOU'VE TRICKED HIM! THAT'S IT! IT'S ALL YOUR FAULT!

IMA- MURA'S—

DON'T LIE TO ME!

MY BOND WITH IMAMURA HAS BEEN FORGED IN THE FIRES OF THE OUENDAN!

OH!

...

HUH? WHAT ARE YOU TWO DOING TOGETHER?

YES, MA'AM!

FLINCH

IMA-MURA!

HELL NO WE'RE NOT DATING!

NO NO NO!

WAVE WAVE

ARE YOU DATING?

CARE TO EX-PLAIN?

YOU NEVER SHOWED UP TO PRACTICE YESTERDAY.

RUMBLE RUMBLE

JUST LET ME DO MY THING!

WH-

WHAT'S IT TO YOU?!

THAT'S ALL HE'S GOT TO SAY?

WHAT HAP-PENED?

I SEE...

...

WAIT!

IMA-MURA-KUN!

SHUK

NO
...

AND THEN, YOU CAN HELP ME WITH MY DO-OVER IN RETURN.

JUST LEAVE IT TO ME.

HEH HEH HEH... I CAN HELP YOU WITH THAT.

ALL YOU WANTED WAS TO GO FURTHER WITH ME, IMAMURA?!

...ALL THE OUENDAN WAS TO YOU?

WAS THAT ...

OH... SEE YOU LATER, THEN.

I'VE GOTTA GO TO THE BATHROOM.

ジロ ホ...

WHAT GIVES?

EVERYONE'S GIVING ME FUNNY LOOKS.

HEY, IMAMURA-KUN.

SMIRK

SMIRK

SMIRK

EXCUSE ME?

IS IT TRUE YOU HAVE A GIRLFRIEND NOW?

HE LEFT SCHOOL WITH A GIRL FROM HIS CLASS TO GO ON A DATE!

YOU HAVEN'T HEARD?

WHAT?!

OH MY GOD!

WAAAA

I HEARD IMAMURA CAME TO SCHOOL WITH HIS GIRLFRIEND TODAY!

DID YOU SEE IT? THE RUMORS WERE TRUE!

UGH!

SHE'S SO UGLY.

WHISPER WHISPER

You're so mean!

CUT THAT OUT!

Ah ha ha ha!

WHAAAT?

Who cares?

I thought he was with the ouendan's captain.

IS SHE REALLY IMAMURA'S GIRL-FRIEND?

I DIDN'T EXPECT PEOPLE TO TALK ABOUT ME LIKE THIS.

FIGURES, THOUGH, I GUESS.

HUH...

CHATTER CHATTER

REALLY?

IS SHIBATA-SAN *THAT* KIND OF GIRL?

WHERE'D IMAMURA AND SHIBATA GO, ANYWAY?

THERE WERE WIT- NESS- ES!

NO WAY!

NOTHING HAPPEN- ED!

I'M TELLING YOU!

So let's stop talking about this! Okay? Okay.

I'M REALLY SORRY, BUT I DON'T WANT TO CAUSE PROBLEMS FOR IMAMURA- KUN, YOU KNOW?

COME ON! JUST GO OUT WITH HIM!

SOUNDS FISHY.

HE'S GETTING IT ON WITH THE CAPTAIN!!

THEY DID THIS TO ME AND THE CAPTAIN, TOO. DON'T THEY EVER SHUT UP?

WHISPER WHISPER

WHISPER

LIS- TEN TO ME!

HMM...

BUT...

SHI-BATA...

I DIDN'T CARE HOW MUCH OF A FUSS THEY MADE THEN, SINCE IT WASN'T LIKE THE CAPTAIN LIKED ME, ANYWAY.

HMM?

HUH!

OH!

DIIING
DOOONG
DAAANG...

GET READY!

ONE, TWO, THREE!

OH, HEY.

THE OUENDAN'S PRACTIC-ING.

I DON'T RECOGNIZE THAT GUY.

WAIT.

SOMEDAY...

I MIGHT GO BACK TO MY OLD WORLD.

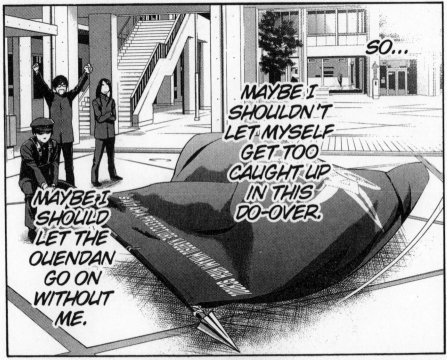

SO...

MAYBE I SHOULDN'T LET MYSELF GET TOO CAUGHT UP IN THIS DO-OVER.

MAYBE I SHOULD LET THE OUENDAN GO ON WITHOUT ME.

AND NOT JUST THE OUENDAN...

NO.

WOBBLE

SHIBATA, TOO.

I PROBABLY SHOULDN'T TAKE THINGS ANY FURTHER WITH HER.

EEP!

BUMP

WEREN'T YOU GOING TO SAY HI TO IMAMURA?

WHAT'S THE MATTER?

HEY, SHI-BATA.

WHAT? NO...

HE LIKES THE CAPTAIN OF THE OUENDAN.

DON'T YOU KNOW THAT?

HE SEEMS SO SAD, WATCHING THE OUENDAN PRACTICE.

WELL, DUH...

JUST LOOK AT HIM.

...

SO YOU DON'T HAVE TO RUB IT IN!

I KNOW I'M NOT THE ONE HE WANTS!

WELL THEN,

LET ME HELP.

I CAN BE A CHEER-LEADER FOR YOUR LOVE.

HUH ...?

WE'RE SUPPOSED TO GO OUT WITH EACH OTHER, HIRO-KUN. REMEMBER?

WHAT MAKES YOU THINK YOU CAN FLIRT WITH HER?

SCRITCH SCRITCH SCRITCH SCRITCH

It's not like they're close... are they?

71. THE ABC'S OF EROS

AND... AND LET'S SEE... THIS ONE. THIS...

Dual's Rokkutei

5F

INTERNET DVD

MANGA CAFÉ

VIDEO

SHUMP
SHUMP
SHUMP
SHUMP

JUST LIKE YOU ASKED. HERE YOU GO.

A KISS THAT CHANGES THE WORLD.

GETTING EXCITED JUST BY HOLDING HANDS.

FATE.

DIFFICULTY EXPRESSING YOUR AFFECTION.

SO THIS IS THE KIND OF MANGA YOU LIKE.

I SEE...

YOUR INNOCENT ACT WON'T WORK ON ME! I KNOW DAMN WELL THAT SMART PEOPLE ONLY EVER THINK ABOUT SEX!

QUIT SCREW-ING AROUND!

YOU'VE GOTTA BE READING DIRTIER STUFF THAN THIS!

YOU SHOULD'VE JUST OWNED UP TO READING THIS STUFF IN THE FIRST PLACE.

I- I'M SORRY.

GOD.

W-WAIT...!

NICE.

UUUNH...

UNH...

MEN ARE SIMPLE CREATURES.

B-BUT, IMAMURA-KUN DOESN'T EVEN LIKE ME.

YOU MAY NOT BE MUCH TO LOOK AT, BUT THAT DOESN'T MEAN HE'D REFUSE YOUR HELP LOSING HIS VIRGINITY!

NOT AN ISSUE!

TUMP

HUH?!

FIRST, YOU NEED TO READ ALL 57 VOLUMES OF KOSAKU SHIMA!

NOW!

GRUMBLE GRUMBLE GRUMBLE

YOU DON'T HAVE TO PUT IT LIKE THAT...

UH, AH...

R-RIGHT.

YOU'RE SMART, SO I KNOW YOU CAN DO IT.

JUST DO AS I SAY, AND YOU'LL UNDERGO A REVOLUTIONARY CHANGE IN PERSPECTIVE.

LIS-TEN.

STRAWBERRY STATEMENT

DIVISION CHIEF KOSAKU SHIMA

HOURS
0 MINUTES
300 YEN

3 HOURS ¥900

6 HOURS ¥1500

7 HOURS ¥1200

10 HOURS ¥1300

DEAL ¥300

AREN'T YOU WORRIED ABOUT HURTING ME?

HOW MUCH TIME DO YOU INTEND TO SPEND TOGETHER?

HIRO-KUN...

GRUMBLE GRUMBLE

GRUMBLE GRUMBLE

REO-CHAN!

HIRO-KUN!

GAH!

GA FÉ

24H OPEN!!

¥900

WHOA!

IT GOT DARK OUT!

GASP

HOW COULD YOU DO THIS TO ME?

IT'S NOT LIKE YOU DON'T KNOW HOW I FEEL ABOUT HIM!

AND COME ON, REO-CHAN! HOW MEAN CAN YOU GET?

WE WEREN'T DOING ANY-THING!

LIAR!

WHAT WERE YOU TWO DOING ALONE TOGETHER IN A MANGA CAFE THIS LATE AT NIGHT?!

NO ONE EVER TOLD ME.

IF I'M NOT SUPPOSED TO SPEND TIME WITH NAKAHARA-KUN BECAUSE YOU LIKE HIM,

COME AGAIN?

WHISPER

NO ONE EVER TOLD ME.

DON'T YOU THINK IT'S A LITTLE PRESUMPTUOUS OF YOU TO JUST ASSUME THAT HE AND I WILL ALWAYS UNDERSTAND HOW YOU FEEL?

R-REO-CHAN?

HUH? WAIT, HOLD ON...

IT'S STARTING TO SEEM SORT OF LIKE YOU'RE STALKING NAKAHARA-KUN.

IN FACT, AKI-CHAN,

YOU SHOULDN'T PUT LIMITS ON LOVE.

DOESN'T IT SEEM SAD TO RESTRICT YOURSELF TO THE WHOLE "BOYFRIEND-GIRLFRIEND" THING?

BLING

MY OLD WORRIES ALL SEEM SO FOOLISH NOW.

IT'S ALL THANKS TO YOU, NAKAHARA-KUN.

YOU'RE SUCH A FAST LEARNER. YOU REALLY ARE THE SMARTEST AT OUR SCHOOL.

GOOD.

SPARKLE

SPARKLE

SPARKLE

JOY

JOY

"LISTEN, SHIBATA. YOU WON'T GET ANYWHERE BY WAITING FOR IMAMURA TO MAKE A MOVE."

CHIRP

CHIRP

WH-WHAT?

HEY, GOOD IDEA.

AHHH! I'D LIKE TO STUDY IN THE USA SO I CAN GET BETTER AT THINKING GLOBAL.

IT SEEMS LIKE LIVING ABROAD WOULD PROBABLY HELP YOU HONE YOUR NATURAL TALENTS.

WHY'D YOU WANT TO MEET HERE FIRST THING IN THE MORNING?

OKAY, SHIBATA. WHAT DO YOU WANT?

HIRO-KUN! WHAT DID YOU DO TO REO-CHAN?

THANKS! ☆

HEH HEH!

"THE ONLY WAY YOU CAN CHANGE HOW HE FEELS IS THROUGH YOUR OWN ACTIONS."

IMA-MURA-KUN,

COME AND KISS ME.

I WANT YOU TO KISS ME RIGHT HERE,

DID YOU HEAR ME?

RIGHT NOW.

SQUEEZE

WHATCHA LISTENING TO?

PRESSSS

HEY, IMA-MURA-KUN!

CHATTER CHATTER...

OH!

...THERE'S THE BELL.

FWOOO

118

HOW ABOUT A ROOFTOP PICNIC, JUST THE TWO OF US?

LET'S EAT, IMA-MURA-KUN!

I MADE US A CUTE LUNCH!

BAM...

STARE...

...

Fwooo

GOTTA CRAP!

YEAH, GOOD IDEA!

LET'S HAVE LUNCH WITH EVERYONE ELSE, INSTEAD.

THAT'S RIGHT, SHIBATA. THINK GLOBAL!

HEH HEH HEH...

YOU'RE MAKING THINGS AWKWARD FOR EVERY-ONE.

WHERE THE HELL IS THIS COMING FROM, SHIBATA?!

SQUEEZE!

?!

HEY!

ACTUALLY, I HAVE TO LOOK AFTER MY GRANDMA. MY MOM WON'T BE HOME UNTIL LATE TONIGHT.

OH, UH...

LET'S GO STRAIGHT TO MY HOUSE AND PICK UP WHERE WE LEFT OFF THE OTHER DAY!

ALL RIGHT!

THIS
IS
BAD.

...

...

...

AND IT'S GONNA GET WORSE IF I END UP ALONE WITH SHIBATA!

He hasn't even married Kumiko Omachi yet!

GAH! I CAN'T READ THE REST OF *KOSAKU SHIMA* WHILE I'M THREE YEARS IN THE PAST!

Again!!
アゲイン!!

72. AN AFTER-HALFTIME AFFAIR

THIS IS NOT THE SHIBATA I KNOW.

CHITTER CHITTER CHITTER CHITTER CHITTER

WHAT THE HELL HAPPENED?!

DON'T TELL ME... DOES SHE WANT TO "PICK UP WHERE WE LEFT OFF" IN MY HOUSE?!

SHE'S OBVIOUSLY LOOKING FOR A CHANCE TO BE ALONE WITH ME.

WHAT HAPPENED TO WAITING UNTIL I WAS READY?!

JUST LET ME KNOW WHEN YOU'RE READY, OKAY?

IMAMURA-KUN,

I WON'T ASK AGAIN.

KIN-CHAN! HIS NAME IS "ELDER KOKONOE" NOW.

Has been for ages.

HEY, GRANDMA, LET'S TURN ON THE TV! THERE'S A SUMO MATCH GOING, AND I KNOW WHAT A FAN YOU ARE OF THAT CHIYONOFUJI GUY.

I'VE GOT TO FIND A WAY OUT OF THIS...

I GOT THE REMOTE!

HE'S STILL IN!

HE'S STILL IN!

WAAA

HE'S GONE IN FOR A LEG HOOK!

WAAA

ALL THIS RACKET SHOULD HELP SPOIL THE MOOD.

Tch.

127

SQUEE

Y-
YOU—

?!

UNH!

MUNCH
MUNCH...

MY GRANDMA'S HERE, FOR CHRISSAKE! HOW STUPID ARE YOU?!

STOP IT!

HAVE SOME SHAME, WOMAN!

THIS ISN'T LIKE YOU AT ALL!

YOU'VE BEEN ACTING WEIRD ALL DAY, SHIBATA!

A LADY DOESN'T PULL THIS KIND OF CRAP.

POINK

LINH
...

LINH
...

...

SHMP

GRANDMA!

BOY, AM I TUCKERED OUT! GOOD NIGHT, KIDS!

ZOOOM

I'M SURE YOU'D BE PERFECTLY HAPPY JUST BEING FRIENDS, WOULDN'T YOU? LINH...

IT'S NOT LIKE YOU LIKE ME OR ANYTHING.

I GET IT.

LINH...

I UNDERSTAND NOW, THOUGH. YOU DON'T FEEL THE SAME WAY AT ALL.

I MEAN— WELL,

...YOU THINK IT'S GROSS THAT I WANT TO DO STUFF LIKE THAT, DON'T YOU?

I BET...

YOU'RE PROBABLY PRETTY ANNOYED THAT WE'RE HAVING THIS CONVERSATION, AREN'T YOU? SORRY...

...

...

SORRY FOR ASSUMING.

÷ SOB ÷

WHAT AM I SUPPOSED TO SAY?!

THE SETUP FOR SOME KIND OF NON SEQUITUR JOKE?

WHAT THE HELL IS THIS?

ABSOLUTELY NOT!

NO!

SHUDDER

WANNA FUCK?

I DIDN'T MEAN TO STRESS YOU OUT. I'M SORRY.

COME ON, SHIBATA. DON'T BE LIKE THAT.

AAAAAGH!

IMA-MURA-

COME ON, SAY SOMETHING.

IMA-MURA-KUN?

GET OVER ME ALREADY, SHIBATA.

IS THIS ME JUST GOING TO SLEEP FOREVER? WILL I DIE?

IF I END UP BACK IN MY OLD LIFE, THREE YEARS IN THE FUTURE... IF I CAN'T COME BACK HERE...

THERE'S NO TELLING HOW MUCH LONGER I'LL GET TO REMAIN IN THIS WORLD.

I DON'T KNOW, BUT WHATEVER!

I'VE ALREADY AC- COMPLISHED MY GOAL OF KEEPING THE OUENDAN ALIVE.

I SHOULD GO BACK TO LIVING IN A WORLD WHERE NO ONE NEEDS ME.

SO THERE'S NO MORE NEED FOR ME TO BE HERE.

MHMM.

CAN I JOIN YOU?

HEY, IMA-MURA-KUN.

...

AFTER ALL, IF I SPEND ANY MORE TIME HERE...

I ND ORE

I'M SORRY. I'M SORRY!

I GOT SO CAUGHT UP IN THAT KISS, I DIDN'T REALIZE.

I THOUGHT YOU WERE TRYING TO KILL ME.

WHA ?!

YOU'RE PRESSING ON MY WINDPIPE ...

THAT HURTS ...

SHI-BATA ...

S-S-SORRY !

KOFF

KOFF

I WAS SCARED THAT YOU HATED ME.

Y'KNOW,

I'VE BEEN WORRIED SINCE I MET YOU, IMAMURA-KUN.

Again!!

アゲイン!!

THE IMAMURA COMEDY HOUR

KIN-CHAAAN!

YOUR CAPTAIN'S HERE!

... UH-

UH-OH. WHAT SHOULD WE DO?

NO ONE TOLD ME!

WH-WHAT'S SHE DOING HERE?!

145

HE'S STILL IN! HE'S STILL IN!

TH- THIS IS CRUEL, IMA-MURA-KUN.

WAIT!

I HID SHIBATA, BUT I FORGOT TO HIDE MYSELF...

I WON'T BE STAYING LONG.

I'M FINE, THANKS.

WHY DON'T YOU HAVE DINNER WITH US?

OH, REALLY? WELL, AT LEAST HAVE SOME TEA BEFORE YOU GO.

HUH. WHERE'S MOM?

SHE WENT TO BED.

OH. SEEMS EARLY, BUT OKAY.

BLUR...

BLUR...

YOU JOINED THE OUENDAN BECAUSE YOU LIKED ME, DIDN'T YOU?

BUT YOU HAD NO REASON TO STICK WITH IT ONCE YOU LOST INTEREST IN ME. SO, YOU'RE QUITTING. AM I WRONG?

...

WOW, SEXIST, MUCH?

JUST 'CAUSE I'M A GUY DOESN'T MEAN I'D MAKE A DECISION LIKE THAT WITH MY DICK!

I MEAN, GET OVER YOURSELF! YOU'RE NOT EXACTLY DRIPPING SEX APPEAL, CAPTAIN!

NO!

IMAMURA-KUN!

YOU TELL HER,

SO YOU DON'T FIND ME ATTRACTIVE AT ALL?

I SEE...

PHEW...

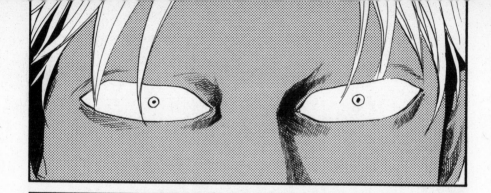

?

HM?

HUUUSH
しーん

SHYMP!

...

SHI-BATA!

THIS IS...

UHH...

WAIT.

SO YOU ARE HERE.

FWISH

YEAH!

ME NEITHER!

YOU DIDN'T FEEL A THING, DID YOU, IMAMURA?

SHAKE

NOPE!

N-

NO, MA'AM!

SHAKE

NO ROMANTIC FEELINGS WILL COME BETWEEN US!

BUT THIS SETTLES IT!

I WAS WORRIED I MIGHT BE FALLING FOR YOU.

THIS IS GREAT!

AND YOU KNOW WHAT THAT MEANS?

WE CAN FORGE A TRUE BOND THAT GOES BEYOND THE ROLES OF MAN AND WOMAN!

THAT WILL BE NECESSARY FOR MY IDEAL OUENDAN!

SO, LET ME GET THIS STRAIGHT.

154

PAT

ぽんっ

PEOPLE LIKE YOU GET SO ADDICTED TO ROMANCE THAT YOU LOSE YOURSELF IN IT.

AS THINGS STAND, YOU'RE NOTHING BUT AN IMPEDIMENT TO IMAMURA.

WHOSE SIDE...

...ARE YOU ON?

TURN

くるっ

HUH?!

...

びくくっ

FLINCH

I NEVER THOUGHT I CARED WHO HATED ME,

BUT DAMN.

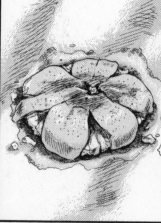

I FEEL LIKE SHIT.

LINH...

I HATE THIS!

LINH...

LILI-LILI-LINH...

LINH...

GOD, IMA-MURA!

YOU'RE SUCH AN ASS-HOLE!

Again!!

アゲイン!!

74.   **THE CREATURE FROM THE WEST BUILDING**

GUH!

ALL SHE DID WAS ACT IN ACCORD WITH HER DESIRES.

IS IT REALLY THAT WEIRD FOR A GIRL TO MAKE A MOVE LIKE THAT?

I'M DISAPPOINTED IN YOU.

LET'S FIGURE OUT HOW TO MAKE SOME CASH!

IMAMURA!

COME ON!

IF SHIBATA DIDN'T DO IT FOR YOU, THEN WHAT'S YOUR TYPE? I'LL FIND YOU A MATCH.

YOU SHOULD FOLLOW YOUR DESIRES LIKE SHE DID.

IN FACT,

GROOON!!

SCRIBBLE

SCRIBBLE

SCRIBBLE

SCRIBBLE

WE DIDN'T HAVE *THAT* MUCH HOMEWORK.

WHAT'S UP, REO? YOU'RE WORKING AWFULLY HARD.

I WANT TO WORK OVERSEAS SOMEDAY,

SO I'VE GOT TO BROADEN MY PERSPECTIVE.

I DON'T WANT TO WASTE MY HIGH SCHOOL CAREER JUST STUDYING FOR EXAMS.

IT'S BORING TO LIMIT MYSELF TO WHAT WE'RE ASSIGNED.

IN THE END, HIRO-KUN DID MANAGE TO CHANGE SHIBATA.

GRRR...

WELL, YOU ALWAYS HAVE BEEN SMART. I'M SURE YOU CAN GO PLACES IF YOU WORK AT IT.

ANYWAY, I PREFER THIS TO HOW WEIRD AND ON-EDGE YOU WERE YESTERDAY.

HUH... YOU'VE STARTED THINKING GLOBAL.

"GLOBAL..."

MUMBLE MUMBLE

WHILE I'M SITTING HERE GOING BACK AND FORTH ON WHETHER I SHOULD HAVE ANYTHING TO DO WITH ANYONE IN THIS DO-OVER WORLD...

...HIRO-KUN COULD BE OUT THERE CHANGING ALL KINDS OF THINGS WITHOUT A SECOND THOUGHT!

...

HEY.

EARTH TO IMAMURA!

I HATE THAT ASS-HOLE!

I HATE HIM SO MUCH!

DO YOU HAVE A MOMENT?

FUJI-EDA?

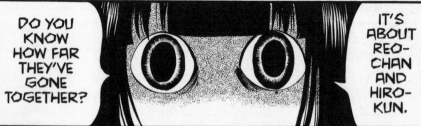

DO YOU KNOW HOW FAR THEY'VE GONE TOGETHER?

IT'S ABOUT REO-CHAN AND HIRO-KUN.

YOU, OF ALL PEOPLE, HAVE TO KNOW SOME-THING, RIGHT? RIGHT?

THEY'RE ALREADY GOING ON KARAOKE DATES, AREN'T THEY?

WHAT?

THAT WOULD BE A PAIN IN THE ASS.

No question.

IF I TELL HER HIRO-KUN JUMPED BACK IN TIME, TOO, SHE'S GOING TO FIND OUT HE DOESN'T LIKE HER.

COME ON!

TELL ME!

SHAKE

SHAKE

SHAKE

YOU LOOK DOWN ON ME, DON'T YOU?

GOD... YOU GET A LITTLE POPULAR IN THE DO-OVER WORLD AND IT GOES STRAIGHT TO YOUR HEAD!

SHIBATA'S NOT THAT KIND OF GIRL.

YOU'RE IMAGINING THINGS, FUJIEDA. NOTHING'S GOING ON BETWEEN THOSE TWO.

SO IT DOESN'T EVEN MATTER WHAT YOU DO HERE, 'CAUSE PRETTY MUCH ANYTHING IS BETTER THAN HOW THINGS WERE.

YOU'RE LUCKY, IMAMURA. YOU DIDN'T HAVE ANYTHING GOING FOR YOU BEFORE. YOU WERE LONELY AND FRIENDLESS.

YOU THINK I'VE LOST IT 'CAUSE I'M THE ONLY ONE WHO HASN'T GOTTEN ANYTHING OUT OF THIS DO-OVER!

YES YOU DO!

NO I DON'T!

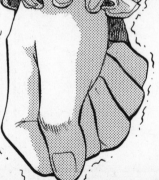

I'M NOT HAVING ANY FUN AT ALL.

...WAS PERMANENTLY RUIN MY LIFE.

BUT ALL DOING THINGS OVER DID FOR ME...

LOOK HOW NEGATIVE I'VE GOTTEN! I NEVER USED TO SAY STUFF LIKE THIS!

IT'S YOUR FAULT, IMA-MURA!

...

HAPPY NOW?

MY BAD.

I MUST BE A REAL MONSTER FOR DOING THAT TO SUCH A POSITIVE PERSON. FOR SHAME.

...

UH-HUH.

YES!

ARE YOU SUG-GESTING MY CYNICISM IS CONTA-GIOUS?

OF COURSE, I WAS ALWAYS A LONER, SO I'M NOT PARTICULARLY ATTACHED TO THE WAY THINGS USED TO BE.

CHANGE ONE THING AND THERE'S NO TELLING WHAT SIDE EFFECTS TO EXPECT.

BUT NOW WE'RE ON A WHOLE DIFFERENT TIMELINE.

I MEAN, I MANAGED TO KEEP THE OUENDAN FROM FALLING APART,

BUT FUJIEDA USED TO HAVE IT ALL. THIS MUST REALLY SUCK FOR HER.

MAYBE I SHOULD THROW MYSELF TO MY DEATH. THEN HIRO-KUN WOULD...

I JUST WANT TO DIE!

HIC!

UNH, UU-UNH!

HOW DO I MAKE MYSELF FEEL BETTER?

UNH...

HGH...

I HATE GETTING ALL HYSTER-ICAL LIKE THIS!

NOOO!

FLINCH

ART CLUB

WHAT'S WITH THIS PILE OF GARBAGE?

IS NOBODY USING THIS ROOM?

WAIT...

SO THIS IS WHERE THE THEATRE CLUB'S ROOM WAS.

IT LOOKS LIKE THEY'RE EVEN DEADER THAN THE OUENDAN WAS, THOUGH.

I NEVER MET ANYBODY WHO WAS IN THIS CLUB.

WHOA!

WHAT A MESS!

OH!

THAT'S IT! I REMEMBER NOW!

JOLT

THERE'S ONE PERSON AT THIS SCHOOL I CAN USE TO MAKE SOME MONEY.

SIGH...

THAT GIRL FROM THE THEATRE CLUB...

I WANT TO DIE.

THIS IS THE AFTERWORD!

The uniform I drew myself wearing in my message on the other side of the front cover of this volume wasn't quite right, actually...

My school's uniform was pretty boring, so once, I dressed up in a uniform I liked instead for an interview for a magazine. That was really fun.

2012.12. 久保ミツロウ☆

Mitsurou Kubo, December 2012

☆ My Agent: Hiromi Sakitani

☆ My Assistants: Shunsuke Ono

Youko Mikuni   Koushi Tezuka

Hiromu Kitano   Kouhei Mihara

Rana Satou

75. NEGATIVITY MONSTER

...IT MUST BE UNBEARABLE TO DO THINGS OVER AND END UP ALL ALONE.

FOR SOMEONE WHO USED TO HAVE IT ALL...

I'm fine, but that's me.

I CAN'T BELIEVE HOW DEPRESSED FUJIEDA'S GOTTEN. SHE USED TO BE SO STUPIDLY HAPPY... I GUESS SHE'S GOING THROUGH A LOT RIGHT NOW.

Before

After

HMM...

I WAS PRETTY HARSH. UGH...

THE CAPTAIN'S RECRUITING NEW MEMBERS TO KEEP THE OUENDAN GOING.

SHIBATA'S FOUND A PURPOSE IN STUDYING SO SHE CAN WORK OVERSEAS.

I MEAN, SINCE WE'RE DOING THINGS OVER, ANYWAY.

SO REALLY, WE JUST NEED TO FIND SOMETHING NEW FOR FUJIEDA TO DO!

THEN AGAIN, IT'S NOT LIKE I'M DOING MUCH.

SO I DOUBT SHE WANTS TO HEAR THAT FROM ME.

HEY HEY HEY HEY! IMAMURA, THIS IS BIG! COME HERE!

SLIDE

HERE SHE IS!

SHE'S IN THE BACK OF THIS PHOTO OF THE THEATRE CLUB FROM THIS GRADUATION YEARBOOK!

THAT'S HER!

I'M TALKING ABOUT TAKA!

YOU DON'T KNOW?

WHO DO YOU MEAN?

SO IT'S TRUE! SHE REALLY WAS IN THE THEATRE CLUB.

SHE WENT TO OUR HIGH SCHOOL!

WAIT...

TAKA? YOU MEAN THE COLLEGE GIRL SEX ICON?!

THAT'S RIGHT!

SHE'S STILL IN HER THIRD YEAR OF HIGH SCHOOL IN THIS WORLD!

BAM

TURNS OUT THE RUMORS WERE TRUE.

I RAN INTO HER OUTSIDE THE THEATRE CLUB ROOM NOT TOO LONG AGO.

YEAH! FOR REAL!

OH MY GOD! ARE YOU SERIOUS?!

THE RUMORS?

BACK THEN, NO ONE EXPECTED HER TO BECOME FAMOUS LIKE THAT.

ME NEITHER!

I NEVER NOTICED HER.

SHE GOT SURGERY. PLASTIC SURGERY.

I MEAN, LOOK. CAN'T YOU TELL?

THEATRE

...

NO WAY! YOU MUST HAVE BEEN SO POPULAR, THOUGH.

HIGH SCHOOL WAS THE WORST.

I THINK I SAW THAT.

OH, HEY!

SHE EVEN WENT ON TV AND TALKED ABOUT HOW SHE WAS SO UNPOPULAR AND UGLY AND USED TO GET BULLIED IN HIGH SCHOOL!

NOT IN THE SLIGHTEST!

HIGH SCHOOL WAS THE WORST...

I WAS CHAIR OF THE THEATRE CLUB, BUT WE DIDN'T HAVE MANY MEMBERS. STILL, THAT WAS THE ONLY PLACE I FELT LIKE I BELONGED.

I THOUGHT ABOUT KILLING MYSELF MORE THAN ONCE.

I GOT BULLIED A LOT BACK THEN.

PEOPLE CALLED ME UGLY, GROSS, EMBARRASSING...

...THAT I'VE GROWN TO BE SO MUCH STRONGER.

AND I THINK IT'S BECAUSE I WENT THROUGH ALL THAT IN HIGH SCHOOL...

THAT'S WHY I HOPE I CAN BE A SOURCE OF COURAGE FOR ANYONE WHO'S HAVING A ROUGH TIME IN SCHOOL NOW.

SHUT UP!

HOW NOBLE!

SHE'S STYLISH, SMART, AND HOT.

AND COOL, TOO.

OH, YEAH? I LIKE HER.

SHE'S TOO OPTIMISTIC. IT'S GRATING.

I HATE TAKA.

IS THIS REALLY ALL YOU HAD?

EH.

DON'T YOU WANT TO KNOW WHAT SHE'S LIKE?

WHAT'S THE POINT OF MEETING HER LIKE THIS?

YEAH, AFTER SHE GETS PLASTIC SURGERY. SHE'S UGLY NOW, THOUGH.

HEH HEH HEH...

...I'M THINKING I MIGHT JOIN THE THEATRE CLUB!

AC-TUALLY...

BAM

HUH?!

SHE'S GOING TO BECOME FAMOUS, SO IF I GET ON HER GOOD SIDE NOW,

THERE COULD BE BENEFITS DOWN THE ROAD!

I WANT TO TRY MY HAND AT CHANGING FATE WITH THIS DO-OVER!

IN FACT...

...YOU COULD SAY I'M GOING TO CHEER THE THEATRE CLUB ON.

FUJI-EDA,

IF *TAKA* HAS TOO GOOD A TIME IN HIGH SCHOOL, ISN'T THAT GOING TO CHANGE HER DESTINY AND KEEP HER FROM BECOMING A STAR?

WHAT?!

184

BACK TO CLASS.

THIS IS WHAT I WANT TO DO! WHY AREN'T YOU CHEERING ME ON?

HEY!

...WHAT'S WRONG WITH THE WAY THINGS ARE?

UH...

SO, I MEAN, IF SHE'S GOING TO END UP HAPPY, ANYWAY...

SHE ONLY BECAME THE TAKA WE KNOW BECAUSE SHE GOT BULLIED IN HIGH SCHOOL, RIGHT?

CLATTER

JUST HOW UGLY IS SHE NOW?

TAKA, HUH?

THAT TAKES SOME GUTS.

AND THE THEATRE CLUB OF ALL THINGS.

HEY! IMAMURA!

185

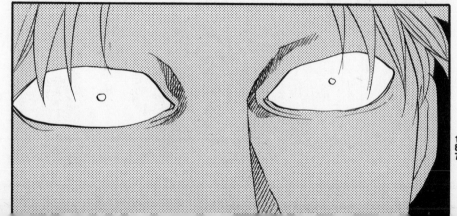

WAAAAAAAAH...!

ACK!

SORRY!

YOU HAVE SOME FACIAL HAIR.

RIGHT THERE.

BLUUUSH

かああっ

GRAB

ズ

I DON'T KNOW.

BY THE WAY, WHAT'S HER REAL NAME?

@TAKA_Destl
this suuuucks.
I want to die *\(^o^)/*
seriously I'm done *\(^o^)/*

TO BE CONTINUED IN VOLUME 8...

IN THE NEXT VOLUME...

SHE SEEMED LIKE THE BOTTOM OF THE BARREL, BUT WHEN SHE LETS DOWN HER HAIR...

SHE'S GOT KIN-CHAN'S HEART BEATING FAST!

MAKES SENSE, THOUGH. IT'S NOT LIKE WE KNOW EACH OTHER.

AT A TIME LIKE THIS...

WHAT MADE MY HEART GO WILD LIKE THAT? I CAN'T LET HIRO-KUN HAVE HIS WAY... BUT I'VE ALREADY BEEN REJECTED...

AND USAMI ENTERS THE FRAY!!!

YOU SHOULD HAVE CALLED THE OUENDAN SOONER, DAMN IT!

IF YOU CAN'T GIVE THE THEATRE CLUB YOUR ALL, WE'LL JUST HAVE TO CHEER YOU ON!

THE OUENDAN'S THEATRE CLUB ARC STARTS NOW!

LIKE IT OR NOT!

Again!!

VOLUME 8 COMING SOON

A Kodansha Comics Trade Paperback Original.

Again!! volume 7 copyright © 2013 Mitsurou Kubo
English translation copyright © 2019 Mitsurou Kubo

Published in the United States by Kodansha Comics, an imprint of Kodansha USA Publishing, LLC, New York.

Publication rights for this English edition arranged through Kodansha Ltd., Tokyo.

First published in Japan in 2013 by Kodansha Ltd., Tokyo, as *Again!!* volume 7.

ISBN 978-1-63236-713-6

Printed in the United States of America.

www.kodanshacomics.com

9 8 7 6 5 4 3 2 1

Translator: Rose Padgett
Lettering: E. K. Weaver
Editing: Paul Starr
Editorial Assistance: Tiff Ferentini
Kodansha Comics edition cover design by Phil Balsman